FAR'S MA GANZIE

Dedicated to the fine people of Northeast Scotland.

Copyright © 2024 Sandra Simpson

All rights reserved.

This book belongs to

Fit like? Foo's yer doo's?

Am Gogsie.

Am scunnered that I've lost ma yella ganzie, i'm jeelt gan aboot wee only ma simmit on. I need to hap mesel up.

Will ye's gee me a han tae find it?

Grunnie, Far's ma yella ganzie?

Is at ma yella ganzie... Grunnie?

'G'wa loon, that's ma cloot fer wiping aff splooters and clarty dubs' said Grunnie.

Yer pechin ma bairn dinna fash yersel, ging and hae a looky in the muckle pile o clise on the lavy fleer.

'It's nae there Grunnie, there's jist the broon eine and I divnae wint the brown eine.' sighed Gogsie.

'I hope ye hinna inter fickered wee the clean clise pile, Gogsie.' Bauled Grunnie fae the Scullery.

Afore it's tatties oer the dyke for ma ganzie I hinna checked one last place...

Hud on a minty, Fit's at keeking oot atween Jocky's dock? Michty me It's ma yella ganzie! Jocky, fit a neep you are, at's nae yer blunky.

Let's nae Clype on Jocky to Ma Grunnie, It was my aine fault for nae pittin awa ma clise. Nae buther said Grunnie pit oan yer yella ganzie and I'll get us ah a fine piece, then we can hae a kick aboot wee the ba.

Translation

(Page 5) Hello? How are you? I am gogsie. (Page 7) I am terribly upset that I have misplaced my yellow sweater. I am cold wearing only my vest. (Page 9) Would you give me some help to find it? (Page 11) Gran, where is my yellow sweater? (Page 13) Is that my yellow sweater upon the counter top Gran? No son that is my dish cloth for cleaning dirt. (Page 15) Please don't worry, why don't you have a look through the laundered clothing on the bathroom floor. (Page 17) Oh gran It's not there I can only see the brown one, but I'd rather not wear the brown one. (Page 19) I hope you have not disrupted the bundle of freshly laundered clothes yelled Gran from the Kitchen. (Page 21) Before I fear my yellow sweater is gone for good. I haven't checked one last place. (Page 23) Alas, wait a minute! What is that peeking through the dog's rear end. Good grief It's my yellow sweater exclaimed Gogsie. What a silly dog you are Jocky, that's not your blanket. (Page 25) Lets not tell tales about Jocky to Mother,Gran, it was my own fault for not tidying my clothes away. Indeed said Gran pop on your yellow sweater and I shall get some cake for us all, then we can play some football.

Written & illustrated by Sandra Simpson

A Local Quine

Printed in Great Britain
by Amazon